THE LORD MY HELPER

79 PRAYER DECLARATIONS

"For HE HIMSELF has said, "I will never leave you nor forsake you." So we may boldly say: "THE LORD IS MY HELPER; I will not fear. What can man do to me?" (Hebrews 13:5-6).

SARAH MORGAN

Copyright © Sarah Morgan
All rights reserved.
ISBN: 978-1-5136-5880-3

MORGAN PUBLISHING

Eliezer The Lord My Helper

Published by Morgan Publishing
888-320-5622

Join the Movement, and Connect with us on:
www.prayeracademy.university
www.prayeracademyglobal.com
www.facebook.com/prayeracademyglobal
www.instagram.com/prayeracademyglobal
www.twitter.com/prayeracademy

All rights reserved. No part of this book may be reproduced or transmitted in any form or by any means without written permission from the author.

PREFACE

HOW TO USE THIS BOOK

The Prayer Declaration Series is designed to strengthen your relationship with God by gaining an awareness of the importance of engaging in prayer for tangible results.

Effective prayer will cause you to soar like an eagle in God's plan for your life. It is a vital key to tapping into the wisdom of God, which will elevate you above mediocrity to produce astounding exploits to the Glory of God.

> *"But the people who know their God shall prove themselves strong and shall stand firm and do exploits [for God]"* (Daniel 11:32).

An intimate prayer life will stabilize and secure every area of your life. Contrary to some opinions, prayer should not be boring. Prayer should be the highlight of your day. Albeit, there is no set way to pray; there are guidelines:

1. Pray to God, the Father, in the name of Jesus Christ.
2. Seek to Establish a Good Personal Relationship with the Lord.
3. Make Sure Your Prayers Always Line Up With the Perfect Will of God for Your Life.
4. Back-Up Your Prayers with Specific Scripture Verses.
5. Do not be Afraid to Write Your Prayers Out to the Lord.
6. Do not be Afraid to go into *Prevailing* Prayer, as Lead by the Holy Spirit.
7. Ask the Holy Spirit to Help You with Your Prayer Life (Romans 8:26).
8. Ask Others to Pray in Agreement with You When Needed.
9. Always Include Prayers of Thanksgiving.
10. Start with Early Morning Prayer and Keep an Ear Tuned to the Holy Spirit Throughout the Entire Day.
11. Read and use the Prayers/Confessions found in the Prayer Declaration Series.
12. Pray in the Holy Spirit. If You have Received the Gift of the Holy Spirit (the language of the Spirit),

you can receive it today. If You Have not received Him, ask; He will fill you. The Gift is Free!

13. Confess Scriptures Straight from the Word.
14. Pray a Scripture from the Word and Expand upon that Prayer, Spontaneously.
15. Pray the Word that is Hidden/Planted in your Heart, Spontaneously.
16. Receive Specific Guidance from the Holy Spirit as to What and How to Pray the Word.
17. Meditate on What You Read From Scripture and Pray the Word from Memory.
18. Pray God's Word and in Your Heavenly Language, and Alternate as the Spirit Leads.

Finally, have a great hunger for God—desperation to pray His will and submit to Him from your heart/spirit. Allow the Holy Spirit to search you. Then, be diligent in crucifying your flesh. Do not be satisfied with self-directed prayer; dig deep into the spirit realm.

When you allow the Holy Spirit to lead you, your spirit will issue, out the forces of life, with effectual fervent prayer. Continue to press into the spirit realm, until your spiritual antennas' tune in to the promptings and leadings of the Holy Spirit. Then as you speak, every stronghold is destroyed, and the power of God released.

When you press into the place of prayer, in the spirit, your spirit becomes one with the Spirit of God. Then, you will pray His desires from your heart, and become intimate with Him, commune with Him, and become lost in Him. It is at that moment; your mind is in total subjection to pray the will of the Father.

Prayer is not forceful but flowing. Prayer is such a great joy that you cannot get enough. May the Spirit of Grace and Supplication fill you to overflowing in the *place of prayer*.

How to Enter into a Time Of Prayer

A.C.T

A - Acknowledge Him for Who He is.
"Know ye that the LORD He is God: it is He that hath made us, and not we ourselves; we are His people, and the sheep of His pasture" (Psalms 100:3).

C – Confess Your Sins, Faults, and Shortcomings.
"If we say that we have no sin, we deceive ourselves, and the truth is not in us. If we confess our sins, he is faithful and just to forgive us our sins, and to cleanse us from all unrighteousness" (1 John 1:8-9).

T - Thanksgiving
"Enter into his gates with thanksgiving, and into his courts with praise be thankful unto him, and bless his name" (Psalms 100:4).

ELIEZER LORD MY HELPER

CONTENTS

	Acknowledgments..	xiii
1	Eliezer God My Helper....................................	1
2	The Power in His Name.................................	5
3	Two Names Associated with God as Our Helper...	15
4	Life is Full of Battles.......................................	21
5	What is a Declaration....................................	29
6	When You Make Declarations.........................	37
7	Prayer Principle of Decoding: When You Pray......	41
8	Prayer Declarations.......................................	47
9	Daily Declarations...	71
10	About the Author...	84

ACKNOWLEDGMENTS

First, to my Abba Father, Pater, Provider, Protector, Preserver, to His Son Jesus and to precious Holy Spirit, my Senior Partner, without this Terrific Trio, I can do nothing. I am eternally grateful and privileged to serve and committed to the cause.

Karla Allen, thank you for editing, formatting, proofing, and helping expedite the process of production. You are a blessing to your generation. I appreciate you.

Sarah Morgan

CHAPTER 1

ELIEZER GOD MY HELPER

*"Let your character be free from the love of money, being content with what you have; for He Himself has said, "I WILL NEVER DESERT YOU, NOR WILL I EVER FORSAKE YOU," so that we boldly say, "THE LORD IS MY **HELPER**, I WILL NOT BE AFRAID. WHAT SHALL MAN DO TO ME?* Jesus Christ the same yesterday, and today, and forever"* (Hebrews 13:5-6, 8).

I want to preface this prayer declaration book with this assurance that God is a Covenant making and a Covenant keeping God.

He made an unconditional Covenant with Abraham:

and thee and thy seed after thee in their generations for an everlasting covenant, to be a God unto thee, and to thy seed after thee. And I will give unto thee, and to thy seed after thee, the land wherein thou art a stranger, all the land of Canaan, for an everlasting possession; and I will be their God" (Genesis 17:7-8).

He affirmed the covenant he made with Abraham, with David:

"My covenant will I not break, nor alter the thing that is gone out of My lips" (Psalm 89:34).

Not only is He a God of Covenant, but He is also a Promise Maker and a Promise Keeper.

*"For all the **Promises of God in Him are yea, and in Him Amen,** unto the glory of God by us" (2 Corinthians 1:20).*

"And it was so, that when Solomon had made an end of praying all this prayer and supplication unto the LORD, he arose from before the altar of the LORD, from kneeling on his knees with his hands spread up to heaven. And he stood, and blessed all the

congregation of Israel with a loud voice, saying, **Blessed be the LORD, that hath given rest unto His people Israel, according to all that He promised: there hath not Failed One Word of All His Good Promise; which He Promised by the hand of Moses His servant.** *The LORD our God be with us, as He was with our fathers:* **let Him not leave us, nor forsake us:"** *(1 Kings 8:54-57).*

There are 365 Promises from God to man in the Bible, which means one promise for each day. Even though God is committed never to break His Covenant Promises concerning covenant sons and daughters, we cannot disregard the fact that between the promise and the fulfillment of the promise, life is full of troubles. Job 14:1 says, *"Man born of a woman of few days, and full of trouble."* The journey of life is never a smooth one, full of struggles, setbacks, battles, and victories, which can only be won by knowing, experiencing, and acknowledging God as a HELPER.

God made Himself known to His people at different stages and phases of their journey by His Covenant and Compound Names.

CHAPTER 2

THE POWER IN HIS NAME

A name is a thing by which a person or thing is known. God is called by many different names in the Bible, each of which reveals aspects of His nature and character.

1. ELOHIM. ELOHIM is the first word used in scripture used to designate "God." "In the beginning, ELOHIM created the heaven and the earth" (Genesis 1:1).

- **EL:** meaning "God, god, mighty one, strength" (Deuteronomy 32:4). EL is usually used in compound with other terms as EL Elyon, EL Shaddai, etc.
- **EL ELYON:** "The Most High" (Deuteronomy 32:8).
- Genesis 14:18-20 KJV – "And Melchizedek king of Salem brought forth bread and wine: and he was the priest of the highest God [EL Elyon]. And

he blessed him, and said, Blessed be Abram of the most high God [EL Elyon], possessor of heaven and earth: And blessed be the most high God [EL Elyon], which hath delivered thine enemies into thy hand."

- **EL OLAM:** "The Everlasting God." Not only is He everlasting in duration, but He is everlastingly faithful.
- Isaiah 26:4 KJV – "Trust ye in the Lord forever: for in the Lord JEHOVAH is everlasting strength."
- **EL SHADDAI:** "The Almighty God."
- Genesis 17:1 KJV – "And when Abram was ninety years old and nine, the Lord appeared to Abram, and said unto him, I am the Almighty God; walk before me, and be thou perfect."
- Some scholars say the word "Shaddai" is derived from the word "Shad," meaning breast, giving rise to the names "The Satisfier" and "All-Sufficient One." Some say "Shad" means "Mountain." Either way, **He is still the God who is more than enough!**

2. **ADONAI: Lord, Master, Owner, Ruler.**

- Used in reference to, men and God - it can refer to a person who is a master, owner, or ruler, or it can refer to the Lord God because He is the Master and Owner of everything.
- When we call Jesus "Lord," we recognize Him as our Master – if we call Jesus Lord and do not obey Him, then our language and conduct are contradicting each other.

3. JEHOVAH: the personal NAME of God in His relationship as REDEEMER.

- Exodus 3:13-15 KJV – "And Moses said unto God, Behold, when I come unto the children of Israel, and shall say unto them, The God of your fathers hath sent me unto you; and they shall say to me, What is his name? what shall I say unto them? And God said unto Moses, I AM THAT I AM: and He said, Thus shalt thou say unto the children of Israel, I AM hath sent me unto you. And God said moreover unto Moses, Thus shalt thou say unto the children of Israel, The Lord God of your fathers, the God of Abraham, the God of Isaac, and the God of Jacob, hath sent me unto you: this is my name forever, and this is my memorial unto all generations."

- Exodus 6:2-3 KJV – "And God spake unto Moses, and said unto him, I am the Lord: And I appeared unto Abraham, unto Isaac, and unto Jacob, by the name of God Almighty, but by my name JEHOVAH was I not known to them."
- Jehovah is the name for the Lord God occurring most frequently in the Old Testament (5,321 times).
- Jehovah is the covenant name of God expressing personal relationship, and when His name is compounded with other terms, together, they identify and make specific those relationships.

4. The Compound Names of JEHOVAH:

JEHOVAH ELOHIM: SUPREME GOD

- Genesis 2:4 KJV – "These are the generations of the heavens and of the earth when they were created, in the day that the Lord God [Jehovah Elohim] made the earth and the heavens."
- **This name identifies Jehovah with the creation of all things. The Triune God is also the Redeemer of His people.**

JEHOVAH JIREH: The LORD will PROVIDE

- Genesis 22:14 AMP – "So Abraham called the name of that place The Lord Will Provide

[Jehovah Jireh]. And it is said to this day, On the mount of the Lord it will be provided."

- God provided a substitute for Isaac, and He provided, for us, once and for all a substitute–the Lamb of God. Romans 8:32 AMP - He who did not withhold or spare [even] His own Son but gave Him up for us all, will He not also with Him freely and graciously give us all [other] things?

JEHOVAH RAPHA: The LORD my HEALER

- Exodus 15:26 NASU – "And He said, "If you will give earnest heed to the voice of the Lord your God, and do what is right in His sight, and give ear to His commandments, and keep all His statutes, I will put none of the diseases on you which I have put on the Egyptians; for I, the Lord, am your HEALER."

- He is speaking here about physical diseases and physical diseases. This promise is conditional upon obedience – yours and mine.

JEHOVAH NISSI: The LORD is my BANNER

- Exodus 17:15 AMP – "And Moses built an altar and called the name of it, The Lord is my Banner. Moses built this altar to commemorate the victory God gave Israel over Amalek. Aaron and Hur had

held up Moses' hands until sunset, and while they did so, Israel prevailed."
- Song of Solomon 2:4 KJV – "He brought me to the banqueting house, and his banner over me was love."

JEHOVAH SHALOM: The LORD is my PEACE

- Judges 6:24 KJV – "Then Gideon built an altar there unto the Lord, and called it Jehovah-shalom. When God called Gideon to lead Israel to victory over the Midianites, the Angel of the Lord appeared to Gideon. When he realized that it was the Angel of the Lord, he thought he would die. The Angel assured him that he would not and spoke peace to him. Jehovah assured him that he would live and lead Israel to triumph. Jehovah was peace to him even before the battles began."
- Shalom (peace) means more than freedom from conflict; it means prosperity, health, well-being, and faith in the face of conflict.
- John 14:27 KJV – "Peace I leave with you, my peace I give unto you: not as the world giveth, give I unto you. Let not your heart be troubled, neither let it be afraid."

JEHOVAH RAAH: The LORD is my SHEPARD

- Psalms 23:1 KJV – "The Lord is my shepherd; I shall not want."
- John 10:11 AMP – "I am the Good Shepherd. The Good Shepherd risks and lays down His [own] life for the sheep."
- 1 Peter 5:4 NKJV – "And when the Chief Shepherd appears, you will receive the crown of glory that does not fade away."

JEHOVAH TSIDKENU: The LORD our RIGHTEOUSNESS

- Jeremiah 23:6 AMP – "In His days Judah shall be saved and Israel shall dwell safely: and this is His name by which He shall be called: The Lord Our Righteousness."
- 1 Corinthians 1:30 KJV – "But of him are ye in Christ Jesus, who of God is made unto us wisdom, and righteousness, and sanctification, and redemption."

JEHOVAH SABAOTH: The LORD of HOSTS

- Psalms 24:10 AMP – "Who is [He then] this King of glory? The Lord of hosts, He is the King of glory."
- 2 Kings 6:13-17 – "Elisha's servant's eyes are opened to see the hosts of God – horses and chariots of fire - surrounding the city."

JEHOVAH SHAMMAH: THE LORD IS THERE

- Ezekiel 48:35 AMP – "The distance around the city shall be 18,000 [4 x 4,500] measures; and the name of the city from that day and ever after shall be, The Lord Is There. God – the great God - is ever present with His people!"

JEHOVAH ELIEZER: THE LORD OUR HELPER

- Hebrews 13:5-6 NKJV – *"For He Himself has said, "I will never leave you nor forsake you." So we may boldly say: "The Lord is my helper; I will not fear. What can man do to me?"*

We are going to know Him as JEHOVAH ELIEZER: THE LORD OUR HELPER. That I May Boldly Say "The LORD Is My Helper."

The **English** word **HELP** means to aid, to lend strength, to Succor to lend a means of deliverance (as to help one in distress), to give assistance (from Latin *ASSISTERE* to STAND BY, from *SISTERE* to CAUSE TO STAND) or support (TO CARRY THE WEIGHT OF, derived from Latin *SUPPORTĀRE* to bring from *sub*-FROM UNDER TO UP ABOVE *PORTĀRE* meaning TO CARRY YOU).

So, HELP means someone who comes to aid,

lend strength, to succor, to lend a means of deliverance (as to help one in distress), to assist, and help in a difficult situation. Someone who will stand by you through adversity, and cause you to stand while supporting you and assisting you by carrying the weight of the holding you up from under, so you can keep your head above water—someone who will sometimes just carrying you through.

Webster says to **HELP** means to assist, to lend strength, or means towards effecting a purpose. To relieve, to cure, or to mitigate pain or disease. To remedy, to change for the better. *Help* means to do for someone what he or she cannot do for himself or herself.

The Hebrew words for Help are:

'Ezer (5828) is a masculine noun which means help, support. It can also refer to a helper or one who assists and serves another with what is needed. For example, in the first OT use where Moses records,

> "*Then the LORD God said, "It is not good for the man to be alone; I will make him a **helper** suitable for him*" (Genesis 2:18).

Azar (5826) means to protect, aid, help, succor, support, give material, or nonmaterial encouragement. **Azar** often refers to aid in the form of military assistance and, in many instances, refers to **help** from Jehovah.

The **Septuagint** translates '**Azar** most often with the word group that conveys the general idea of running to the aid of one who cries out for help which is similar to the English word **succor** (from Latin *succurrere* meaning to run up, run to help) **means literally to run to support, to go to the aid of, to help or relieve when in difficulty, want or distress; to assist and deliver from suffering; as, to succor a besieged city; to succor prisoners.**

Ezrah (5833) means help, support, assistance, aid, either human or divine. It is often used in the sense of a helper or assistant, one who assists and serves another with what is needed.

The **Greek words** that are most often used in the **Septuagint (LXX)** to translate the preceding Hebrew words are:

Boetheia describes the assistance offered to meet a need. In secular Greek, this word was used to describe a medical aid or a cure.

Boethos it the noun form of the verb boetheo and describes one who runs on hearing a cry to give assistance. It is used once in the NT as a description of God our Helper. (Hebrews 13:6)

CHAPTER 3

TWO NAMES ASSOCIATED WITH GOD AS OUR HELPER

1. **ELIEZER - GOD IS MY HELP:**
    a. **ELIEZER** is composed of two words **El** = God and **EZER** = help, and means, in essence, **"God is his help."**
    b. **ELIEZER** is found 15 times in Scripture, describing 11 individuals. Still, the most definitive description is by Moses, who records that one of his two sons by Zipporah was named **ELIEZER**, for he said, "The **God** (Elohim) of my father was my **Help** (Ezer) and delivered me from the sword of Pharaoh." (Exodus 18:4)
    c. **Eliezer** (from '**El** means God or '**Eli** means my God + 'Ezer is help) means "***God is help,*** " "***my God is help,***"

"God of help," "God is (his or my) help" or *"My God is (a) Helper"* (the specific translation depending on which Bible dictionary you consult).

In short, Moses' named his son Eliezer, a testimony reflecting his personal experiences with God His Helper. Every time Moses called out Eliezer's name, he would be saying, "**God is my Helper.**"

Likewise, every time we go through the different challenging seasons of our lives, and we experience the divine intervention of God, we too can call on Eliezer declaring, **"God is our Helper."**

May you know God as Eliezer; God your Helper.

2. **EBENEZER MY STONE OF HELP:**
    a. **EBENEZER** is derived from two words, **EBEN,** meaning stone, and **EZER,** meaning help and thus means **"STONE OF HELP."**
    b. Then Samuel took a stone ('Eben) and set it between Mizpah and Shen, and named it **Ebenezer (literally "Stone of Help")**, saying, "**Thus far Jehovah has helped us.**" 1 Samuel 7:12 **"Hitherto hath the Lord HELPED US"**

The signification of the word "stone" in a broad sense is truth, concerning facts we see. Stones have signified truth for the reason that the boundaries of the most ancient people were marked off by stones. Stones were also set up as witnesses that a case was so and so, or that it was true; as evident from the stone that Jacob set up for a pillar (*Gen*esis 28:22; 35:14), and from the pillar of stones between Laban and Jacob (*Gen*esis 31:46, 47, 52), and the altar built by the sons of Reuben, Gad, and Manasseh, near the Jordan, as a witness (*Josh*ua 22:10, 28, 34).

As then in ancient times truths were signified by stones, and afterward when worship began upon pillars and altars, and in a temple, holy truths were signified by the pillars, altars, and temple; therefore the Lord also was called A Stone; as in Moses:--

The Mighty One of Jacob, from thence is the Shepherd, the Stone of Israel (*Gen*esis 49:24). "*Thus saith the Lord Jehovah, Behold, I lay in Zion for a foundation a Stone, a tried Stone of the corner, of price, of a sure foundation*" (*Isaiah 28*:16).

> *So the people said to Joshua, "We will serve the LORD our God and obey His voice." On that day Joshua made a covenant for the people, and*

there at Shechem he established for them a statute and ordinance. Joshua recorded these things in the Book of the Law of God. Then he took a large Stone and set it up there under the oak that was near the sanctuary of the LORD. And Joshua said to all the people, **"You see this Stone. It will be a witness against us, for it has heard all the words the LORD has spoken to us, and it will be a witness against you if you ever deny your God"** *(*Joshua 24:24-27).

The Stones have memory (matter has memory); they are a memorial, and they bear witness of everything, especially the times when God has been Ebenezer, our Stone of Help.

So, when Jesus said to the people as He entered Jerusalem riding on a donkey and the religious community tried to silence the people, *"I tell you,"* He answered, *"if they remain silent, the very stones will cry out."* Luke 19:40

Jesus was reminding them that the Stones were a memorial; they had memory of the many times that The Lord had Helped Israel and were grateful for this day because the promise of it had been recorded, and they would bear witness hence cry out.

Don't let the stones in your memorial walls, whether generational, ancestral, family, or relational cry out for or against you, as long as you have breath in you, and are still in the land of the living.

The stone Samuel named Ebenezer was a memorial to help Israel remember the many past incidents of **Jehovah's HELP**. Imagine every time the Lord helps us, we mark it with a memorial stone saying, **"Hitherto hath the Lord HELPED us,"** we would build a fortified impenetrable wall of defense.

Though God is Ebenezer, our Stone of Help in this book, our Declarations will be directed to Jehovah ELIEZER, The LORD is my HELPER.

CHAPTER 4

LIFE FULL OF BATTLES

Even though God is committed never to break His Covenant Promises concerning His covenant sons and daughters, we cannot disregard the fact that between the promise and the fulfillment of the promise, life is full of troubles. Job 14:1 says, "*Man born of a woman of few days, and full of trouble.* Some people have described life as a battleground. Why? Because you and I have to fight many battles to survive and thrive, no one can effectively traverse the terrain of life and advance triumphantly without doing some form of battle.

A wise man once said that from the day a baby is born, leaving the safe environment of his mother's womb, he comes out with his little fingers clenched in a fist because he has to fight the inevitable environment the world has to offer. He comes out fighting the hostile environment of all kinds of germs and diseases, alien to the safely protected womb of his mother, hence the need to take so many immunization shots just to protect him from potential harm to grow up healthy. Growing up as a child, he needs to fight for the attention and recognition of his existence; he has to fight for acceptance, peer pressures, and the favor of contemporaries. Education at every level is a fight, entering the job market to establish a career is a fight, navigating love, life and settling down is a fight and many more hurdles he has to overcome just to survive.

Likewise, as a covenant child of God spiritual growth is also a battle, ever since the great fall, men have to fight to resist the fallen, corrupted nature, temptation from the inside and out, crossing rivers of evil all over, climbing mountains of human deficiency and continuously fight the spiritual war against the devil every day of his life. No one was born with a godly inclination. We all were born with a tendency of a downhill spiral of spiritual deprivation.

"Behold, I was shapen in iniquity; and in sin did my mother conceive me" (Psalm 51:5).

The LORD HELPS Fight Our Many Battles:
In times of **battle,** sometimes the believer's only prayer is, **"Help us, LORD."**

"Then Asa called to the LORD his God and

*said, "**Jehovah**, there is no one besides You to **help** in the **battle** between the powerful and those who have no strength; so **HELP** us, O LORD our God, for we trust in You, and in Your name have come against this multitude. O LORD, You are our God; let not man prevail against You" (2 Chronicles 14:11).*

MANY BATTLES MANY ENEMIES

First, you must be aware that there is more than one enemy. There are many enemies, a multitude.

"And shall say unto them, Hear, O Israel, ye approach this day unto battle against your enemies: let not your hearts faint, fear not, and do not tremble, neither be ye terrified because of them; For the LORD your God is He that goeth with you, to fight for you against your enemies, to save you" (Deuteronomy 20:3-4).

*"Then Zerah the Ethiopian came against them with an army of **1,000,000 men and 300 chariots,** and they advanced as far as Mareshah" (2 Chronicles 14:9).*

*"Then Asa cried out to the LORD his God: "O LORD, there is no one besides You **to help the***

powerless against the mighty. Help us, *O LORD our God, for we rely on You, and in Your name we have come against this **multitude**. O LORD, You are our God. Do not let a mere mortal prevail against You" (2 Chronicles 14:11).*

A Multitude, Army, Host, Legion; These nouns denote a large number of people or things that have some attribute in common or that operate together as a larger unit that invades you and your environment with the intent to cause harm and destruction.

ELIEZER Help Us Overcome this Multitude:

*"So **HELP** us, O LORD our God, for we trust in You, and in Your name have come against this **multitude**" (2 Chronicles 14:11).*

Secondly, battles and enemies need no invitation. They will come to you anytime, anywhere they choose to without warning. The children of Israel in the Bible from Egypt to Canaan encountered many enemies. The Amalekites, the Philistines, the Edomites, the Ammonites, and the Midianites were all the enemies they faced, just to mention a few.

The same happens in real life today. Challenges and

hurdles are part of everyday life. Problems and difficulties are a part of every human being. Count it not strange by the number of enemies or battles you may have at one time or another.

In Exodus 17:1-7, while the Israelis were peacefully traveling, finding their way out of the land of oppression and slavery, the Amalekites decided to come and attacked them without warning or reason. *"Then came Amalek, and fought with Israel in Rephidim" (Exodus 17:8).*

You don't have to do anything wrong, to provoke anyone's anger, or to be blamed for anything. Problems, betrayal, criticism, let downs, and unfair treatments will find their way to you. That is life, and we can do nothing about it.

Thirdly, battles come in many forms. Physical battles may be brutal but are easy to recognize and fight. Battles that are external or extrinsic are easier to be identified. But there are enemies and battles you never imagine they will come, but they do; the internal or intrinsic, proximity, least expected from covert battles. I don't mean you need to be suspicious of all the people around you. What I am trying to say is DO NOT be surprised if one of your "friends" turned out to be your fearful enemy someday. People whom you trust the most might one day lift his heel against you as David had lamented. (Psalm 41:9)

DIFFERENT KINDS OF BATTLES

3. Battles of the FLESH and evil nature of man.
4. Battles of the HEART, the greed, hatred, and wicked thoughts of man.
5. Battles of the WORLD or worldly values and pleasure-seeking lifestyle.
6. Battles in RELATIONSHIPS
7. Battles in your MARRIAGE
8. Battles in your HEALTH
9. Battles with your CHILDREN
10. Battles with your FINANCES
11. Battles with TEMPTATIONS
12. Battles with WORRY
13. Battles with your LONELINESS
14. Battles with LUST AND SEXUAL IMPURITY
15. Battles with PRIDE
16. Battles with BARREN-NESS
17. Battles with GRIEF AND SORROW

We are always at war battling against the devil, the world, and our corrupted nature. But, take heart you are not fighting alone, Jehovah Eliezer, the Lord who

HELPS, will help you overcome because He is a Promise maker and a Promise Keeper.

> *"Let your character be free from the love of money, being content with what you have; for He Himself has said,* ***"I WILL NEVER DESERT YOU, NOR WILL I EVER FORSAKE YOU,"*** *so that we* ***BOLDLY*** *(confidently) say,* ***"THE LORD IS MY HELPER, I WILL NOT BE AFRAID. WHAT SHALL MAN DO TO ME"*** *(Hebrews 13:5-6).*
>
> **vs 8** *"Jesus Christ the same yesterday, and today, and forever."*

IN THIS BOOK WE WILL DECLARE JEHOVAH ELIEZER IS THE LORD OUR HELPER.

CHAPTER 5

WHAT IS A DECLARATION?

The English word "Declare" comes from the Latin word Declarare, the root being Clarus, which means "clear" and "de," which means "Thoroughly." **Thus "To Declare" means "To Make Thoroughly Clear."**

A Declaration means, **"To say something in an emphatically, proclaim, tell, formally announce, state, assert, affirm something that is, make known, reveal."**

The primary Hebrew word translated **"Declare"** is nagad, and there are several of Greek words translated **"Declare"** in the NASB meaning:

1. To announce (Luke 8:47; John 4:23).
2. To order, command (Acts 17:30).
3. To announce, report (Acts 20:27).
4. To say the same word, to confess (Matthew 7:23).
5. To speak out (Acts 2:14).
6. To cry out (Acts 25:24).
7. To divide, separate, designate (Romans 1:4).

The root of (1), (2), and (3) is Angello, which means "Message," and is the root of the English word "Angel," which means "Messenger." In Biblical terms, a **"Declaration"** is a message or a word, spoken or written, which makes known the truth about something.

Countries make a "Declaration of war," which means that they make known that a state of war now exists. When a person enters a country, a customs agent requires the person to "Declare" what they are bringing into the country, which means they are to make known and reveal what they have in their possession.

While declarations can be and are to be an essential aspect of prayer, in the general sense, speaking to God, in the restricted sense of the definition of prayer, a declaration is not a prayer because it is not a petition—asking God for something one needs or desires.

To declare, however, is to make something known, to acknowledge what exists, to proclaim the truth of what is. For example, concerning God, Deuteronomy 4:13 states, "So He declared (nagad) to you His covenant which He commanded you to perform, that is, the Ten Commandments; and He wrote them on two tablets of stone." God made known the covenant and terms of the covenant that He established between

Himself and His people.

In the general sense of prayer, when one confesses their sins to God, they make known and acknowledge the truth of what has existed, which is that they have sinned. Then, in the more restrictive sense, one prays and asks God to forgive their sins.

To "Declare," God's word is to make known or acknowledge the truth of what God has revealed in His word concerning a matter. Such a declaration does not create a new reality. It acknowledges and makes known what already is reality.

A change can take place in someone who hears it. However, this is simply a change in their awareness and comprehension of that truth, not a difference in the reality of what has been declared. Thus, a declaration does not create something or bring into existence that which it declares, other than the awareness and alignment of someone's comprehension of it. It is, in essence, a word about what already exists, the truth about what is. So, when God says in His word.

"Fear not I Am with thee, be not dismayed, I Am Your God, I Will HELP thee, I will strengthen thee, I will uphold thee with My Right hand of righteousness" (Isaiah 41:10).

Such a declaration is not creating a new reality. It's acknowledging and making known what already is reality. **IT'S A STATEMENT OF FACT! A DECLARATION!**

"For He Himself has said, I will Never leave you, nor will I ever Forsake you, that you might say, **The LORD is my HELPER [ELIEZER],** *I will not be afraid, what can man do to me"* (Hebrews 13:5-6).

Such a declaration is not creating a new reality. It's acknowledging and making known what already is reality**. IT'S A STATEMENT OF FACT! A DECLARATION!**

Therefore, to declare and proclaim God's word is to make known the truth about **what God has already said, which the truth is.** God said **I Will HELP you**, is a statement of truth **so you "Declare" The Lord is my Helper, He will HELP me. POWERFUL!**

To declare the glory of God is to make known what already an established truth is and to proclaim the reality of it. **The Psalms are full of declarations concerning the truth of who God is, what He has done, is doing and will do.**

Psalm 9:11 says, *"Declare among the peoples*

His deeds," and Psalm 19:1 states, *"The heavens are telling of the glory of God; and their expanse is declaring the work of His hands."*

How does all this relate to prayer, you may ask? So, when a declaration is directed toward God, it becomes an Aspect of Prayer in the general sense because it is now speaking to God. When you pray SAY; "Our Father" (Luke 11:2), Jesus taught where to direct prayer, To the Father. So, the last statement of that model, Lord's Prayer, is not a prayer request, but a declaration: "For Yours is the Kingdom, the Power, and the Glory" (Matthew 6:13).

The first part and most of the prayer of the church recorded in Acts 4:24-28 in response to persecution began with declarations.

THE DECLARATIONS:

- **Act 4:24** – "And when they heard that, they lifted up their voice to God with one accord, and said, Lord, thou *art* God, which hast made heaven, and earth, and the sea, and all that in them is:"
- **Act 4:25** – "Who by the mouth of thy servant David hast said, Why did the heathen rage, and the people imagine vain things?"

- **Act 4:26** – "The kings of the earth stood up, and the rulers were gathered together against the Lord, and against his Christ."
- **Act 4:27** – "For of a truth against thy holy child Jesus, whom thou hast anointed, both Herod, and Pontius Pilate, with the Gentiles, and the people of Israel, were gathered together."
- **Act 4:28** – **"For to do whatsoever thy hand and thy counsel determined before to be done."**

It is then after the declarations were made that the requests, or prayer in the restricted sense, are offered in verses 29-30.11.

The REQUEST and PRAYER PETITION

- **Act 4:29 – "And now, Lord, behold their threatenings: and grant unto thy servants, that with all boldness they may speak thy word."**
- **Act 4:30 – "By stretching forth thine hand to heal; and that signs and wonders may be done by the name of thy holy child Jesus."**

THE RESPONSE

- **Act 4:31 – "And when they had prayed, the place was shaken** where they were assembled together; and they were all filled with the Holy Ghost, and they spake the word of God with boldness."

Declarations do not create something about God or a new reality but acknowledge and proclaim the truth about Who He is and what He has done and declared the ability to do.

As a believer, you can make declarations to make known these truths. Declarations can be spoken to God as a part of corporate prayer gatherings, in the general sense, as an aspect of worship or witness, and to the spirit realm.

You can, in effect, clear, establish and align the spiritual atmosphere of a particular place and environment by making declarations concerning the truth of Who God is what Christ has done, Who Christ now is, and what He will do, as well as who they are in Christ.

You can declare to the satanic spirits the truth about who and what they are in Christ and Christ's victory and dominion over Satan and His kingdom. Jesus said, *"Hereafter I will not talk much with you: for the prince of this world cometh, but he has nothing in me." John 14:30* Such a declaration was not creating a new reality. It was acknowledging and making known what was already a reality.

IT WAS A STATEMENT OF FACT! A DECLARATION! THAT ALTHOUGH HE COMETH, BUT HE HAS NOTHING IN ME!

In making these declarations, as a believer you do not create something new or bring into existence a new reality but rather you orient, bring a shift and align yourself and the spiritual realm to and with the truth of God as it is revealed in His word.

While, as a believer, you have a delegated authority in Christ, the source of authority of such declarations is not the person making the declaration but God Himself Who has given and revealed His word in Scripture.

Declarations have the power to increase our level of faith to propel us to experience all that Jesus has won for us. *"Faith comes by hearing,"* (Romans 10:17).

You won't have something just by saying something but saying something is necessary to having something, which means "messenger." *"When you pray SAY."* To declare is to make something known, to acknowledge what exists, to proclaim the truth of what is.

CHAPTER 6

WHEN YOU MAKE DECLARATIONS

As You Pray And Make These Declarations, Believe, Trust And Be Confident, Of These Truths:

1. **Know that God is with you.**

   Many believers have no confidence in God because they don't understand that God is with them. Hebrews 13:5 says that God will **never** leave us or forsake us. God is Omni-Present, always present everywhere, every time. Whether you feel it or not, believe it or not, He is!

   When God says, "I will **never**," He means never because It's His attribute and nature. Like Asa for the prayer of Eliezer, the Lord our Helper, to work, you must believe that He IS with you and will **NEVER** leave you nor forsake you.

2. **So that we may boldly SAY: You will have what you SAY.**

   "God will never leave us or forsake us. The next

verse begins, *"SO THAT we may BOLDLY say, **the Lord is my HELPER,** and I will not fear"* (Hebrews 13:5).

To be bold is to be daring and fearless, in the confidence that the Lord is with us, hence the writer is admonishing us that our approach and declaration that **Eliezer "The Lord Is our Helper,"** must be daring and fearless in the face of adversity. The power is in your mouth; the power is in what you say. Jesus taught His disciples, *"When you Pray, SAY" (Luke 11:2).*

*"Truly I say unto you that if anyone says to this mountain, 'Be lifted up and cast into the sea,' and does not doubt in his heart but believes that it will happen, he will have what he **says"** (Mark 11:23).*

*"Then Asa cried out to the LORD his God: "O LORD, there is no one besides You to HELP the powerless against the mighty. **HELP us, O LORD our GOD, for we rely on You,** and in Your Name we have come against this Multitude. O LORD, You are our God. Do not let a mere mortal prevail against You (2 Chronicles 14:11).*

"And because they cried out to God in

battle, ***they were HELPED against their enemies,*** *and the Hagrites and all their allies were delivered into their hands. Because they put their trust in God, He answered their prayers" (1 Chronicles 5:20).*

Their declaration that Eliezer "The Lord Is our **HELPER**" was daring and fearless in the face of adversity, and in the face of the multitude who were mighty mentally, emotionally, physically, psychologically, relationally, socially, economically, generationally, morally, and spiritually.

CHAPTER 7

Prayer Principle of Decoding: When You Pray

1. **ACKNOWLEDGE HIS SOVEREIGNTY AND ULTIMATE ABILITY TO HELP YOU.**

O LORD, You are our God. Do not let a mere mortal prevail against You.

> *"Now to him who is **Able to do** immeasurably more than all we ask or imagine, according to his power that is at work within us"* (Ephesians 3:20).

> *"God can do anything, you know—far more than you could ever imagine or guess or request in your wildest dreams! He does it not by pushing us around but by working within us, his Spirit deeply and gently within us"* (Ephesians 3:20 MSG).

2. **ACKNOWLEDGE THAT YOU ARE POWERLESS WITHOUT HIS POWER.**

O LORD, there is no one besides You to HELP the powerless.

> *"He gives strength to the weary and increases the power of the weak"* (Isaiah 40:29).

> *"One thing God has spoken, two things I have heard: Power belongs to you, God"* (Isaiah 62:11).

3. **ACKNOWLEDGE THAT THE ENEMIES YOU'RE FACING ARE MANY AND MIGHTY.**

> *We have come against this Multitude!*

The multitude who are many mentally, emotionally, physically, psychologically, relationally, socially, economically, generationally, morally, and spiritually;

4. **ACKNOWLEDGE THAT YOUR TOTAL RELIANCE IS ON HIM AND HIS NAME.**

HELP us, O LORD our GOD, for we rely on You, and in Your Name we have come against this Multitude.

"This is the confidence (the assurance, the privilege of boldness) which we have in Him:[we are sure] that if we ask anything (makes you request) according to His will (in agreement with His own plan), He listens to and hears us" (1 John 5:14).

1 John 5:15, "And if we know that He hears us, whatever we ask, we know that we have the petitions that we have asked of Him."

John 14:14, "If you ask anything in my name, I will do it."

John 14:13, "And whatever you ask in My name, that I will do, that the Father may be glorified in the Son."

"Let us therefore come boldly to the throne of grace, that we may obtain mercy and find grace to HELP in time of need." Hebrews 4:6 (KJV)

"Therefore let us confidently approach the throne of grace to receive mercy and find grace whenever we need HELP." Hebrews 4:6 (Net Bible)

The next verse begins**, "SO THAT we may boldly Say, "*The Lord is my helper, and I will not fear!*"**

In other words, since, indeed, God will never leave or forsake us, that means God is with us. He's on our side, and He's with us to Help us! We can have confidence in that! No matter where we are in life, we should be faithful to give thanks to the Lord because He is our Helper.

If we're facing a need or a problem today, we can thank God that He delivers us out of trouble. If we are enjoying abundance today, let us remember that we had His help getting to that place in life.

"The Lord is my HELPER, and I will not Fear."

WHEN YOU CALL ON ELIEZER THE LORD IS MY HELPER, THERE IS NO FEAR.

"Fear thou not; for I am with thee: be not dismayed; for I am thy God: I will strengthen thee; yea, I will help thee; yea, I will uphold thee with the right hand of my righteousness" (Isaiah 41:10).

The struggles, setbacks, battles, and victories of God's people in the Bible are the same for modern-day Christians. **I want you to know that God IS the same yesterday, today, and forever He is still a Helper, and He will Help you.**

"Jesus Christ the same yesterday, and today,

and forever" (Hebrew 13:8).

With Jehovah Eliezer God, our HELPER, I Declare:

*"The Lord is my strength and my strong **Helper** He has become my salvation: He is my God and I will give Him praise; my father's God and I will give Him glory" (Exodus 15:2).*

*"Thou hast seen it; for thou beholdest mischief and spite, to requite it with thy hand: the poor committeth himself unto thee; thou art the **Helper** of the fatherless" (Psalm 10:14 [BBE]).*

"But the salvation of the righteous is of the LORD: **He is their strength in the time of trouble. And the LORD shall Help them, and deliver them***: He shall deliver them from the wicked, and save them, because they trust in Him" (Psalm 37:39-40).*

*"I am oppressed and needy! May the Lord pay attention to me! You are my **Helper** and my deliverer! O my God, do not delay!" (Psalm 40:17* [NET]*).*

"God is our refuge and strength, a very

*present **Help** in trouble" (Psalm 46:1).*

*"Behold, God is my **Helper**; The Lord is the sustainer of my soul" (*Psalm 54:4*).*

*"If the LORD had not been my **Helper**, I would have quickly become silent. Psalm 94:17* [ISV] *The Lord is my **Helper**, Therefore, I will look in triumph on those who hate me" (Psalm 118:7*[HCSB]*).*

*"Have no fear, for I am with you; do not be looking about in trouble, for I am your God; I will give you strength, yes, I will be your **Helper;** yes, my true right hand will be your support" (Isaiah 41:10* [BBE]*).*

*"I will lift up mine eyes unto the hills, from whence cometh my help. **My Help cometh from the LORD,** which made heaven and earth" (*Psalm 121:1-2*).*

IN THIS BOOK WE WILL BE DECLARING JEHOVAH ELIEZER IS THE LORD OUR HELPER.

Declarations have the power to increase our level of faith to propel us to experience all that Jesus has won for us. *"Faith comes by hearing,"* (Romans 10:17).

CHAPTER 8

Prayer declarations

WITH JEHOVAH ELIEZER GOD OUR HELPER, I DECLARE:

*"With him is an arm of flesh; but with us is the **LORD our God to HELP us, and to FIGHT our BATTLES**. And the people rested themselves upon the words of Hezekiah king of Judah" (2 Chronicles 32:8).*

With Jehovah ELIEZER, God our HELPER, I Declare He will help me fight the Battles of the FLESH, the evil nature of man, and overcome them.

1. **With Jehovah ELIEZER, God our HELPER, I Declare that though my flesh and heart fail, God is my strength and portion forever.**

    "My flesh and my heart faileth: but God is the strength of my heart, and my portion forever" (Psalm 76:26).

2. **With Jehovah ELIEZER, God our HELPER, I Declare I am not under condemnation, but I am in Christ Jesus.**

   "There is therefore now no condemnation to them which are in Christ Jesus, who walk not after the flesh, but after the Spirit. For the law of the Spirit of life in Christ Jesus hath made me free from the law of sin and death" (Romans 8:1-2).

3. **With Jehovah ELIEZER, God our HELPER, I Declare Christ condemned my sin through His death in the flesh.**

   "For what the law could not do, in that it was weak through the flesh, God sending his own Son in the likeness of sinful flesh, and for sin, condemned sin in the flesh" (Romans 8:3).

4. **With Jehovah ELIEZER, God our HELPER, I Declare I no longer walk after the flesh, but after the Spirit.**

   "That the righteousness of the law might be fulfilled in us; who walk not after the flesh, but after the Spirit" (Romans 8:4).

5. **With Jehovah ELIEZER, God our HELPER, I Declare I no longer mind the things of the**

flesh but of the Spirit.

"For they that are after the flesh do mind the things of the flesh; but they that are after the Spirit the things of the Spirit" (Romans 8:5).

6. **With Jehovah ELIEZER, God our HELPER, I Declare I am no longer a debtor to my flesh.**

"Therefore, brethren, we are debtors, not to the flesh, to live after the flesh" (Romans 8:12).

7. **With Jehovah ELIEZER God our HELPER, I Declare, through the Spirit of God, I do mortify my flesh.**

"For if ye live after the flesh, ye shall die: but if ye through the Spirit do mortify the deeds of the body, ye shall live" (Romans 8:13).

8. **With Jehovah ELIEZER, God our HELPER, I Declare I am led by the Spirit of God, and I am a child of God.**

"For as many as are led by the Spirit of God, they are the sons of God" (Romans 8:14).

9. **With Jehovah ELIEZER, God our HELPER, I Declare I have not received the spirit of bondage again to fear.**

"For ye have not received the spirit of bondage again to fear; but ye have received the Spirit of adoption, whereby we cry, Abba, Father" *(Romans 8:15).*

10. **With Jehovah ELIEZER, God our HELPER, I Declare I have received the Spirit of adoption, whereby I cry, Abba Father.**

"For ye have not received the spirit of bondage again to fear; but ye have received the Spirit of adoption, whereby we cry, Abba, Father" *(Romans 8:15).*

11. **With Jehovah ELIEZER, God our HELPER, I Declare I am a child of God.**

"The Spirit itself beareth witness with our spirit, that we are the children of God" *(Romans 8:16).*

12. **With Jehovah ELIEZER, God our HELPER, I Declare I am an heir of God and a joint-heir with Christ not after the flesh but after the spirit.**

"And if children, then heirs; heirs of God, and joint-heirs with Christ; if so be that we suffer with Him, that we may be also glorified together" *(Romans 8:17).*

13. **With Jehovah ELIEZER, God our HELPER, I Declare I have put on the Lord Jesus Christ.**

"But put ye on the Lord Jesus Christ, and make not provision for the flesh, to fulfil the lusts thereof" (Romans 13:14).

14. **With Jehovah ELIEZER, God our HELPER, I Declare I will no longer make provision for the flesh, to fulfill the lusts of thereof.**

"But put ye on the Lord Jesus Christ, and make not provision for the flesh, to fulfil the lusts thereof" (Romans 13:14).

15. **With Jehovah ELIEZER, God our HELPER, I Declare I do not war after the flesh, for my weapons are not fleshy but spiritual and mighty in God.**

"For though we walk in the flesh, we do not war after the flesh: (For the weapons of our warfare are not carnal, but mighty through God to the pulling down of strong holds;)" (2 Corinthians 10:3-4).

BATTLES OF THE HEART, THE HATRED AND THE EVIL THOUGHTS OF MAN.

16. **With Jehovah ELIEZER, God our HELPER, I Declare that my heart will not be defiled, and all evils will not proceed from it.**

"And He said, "What comes out of a man that defiles a man. For from within, out of the heart of men, proceed evil thoughts, adulteries, fornications, murders, Thefts, covetousness, wickedness, deceit, lasciviousness, an evil eye, blasphemy, pride, foolishness: All these evil things come from within, and defile the man" (Mark 7:20-22).

17. **With Jehovah ELIEZER, God our HELPER, I Declare I shall love the Lord with all my heart.**

"And thou shalt love the LORD thy God with all thine heart, and with all thy soul, and with all thy might" (Deuteronomy 6:5).

18. **With Jehovah ELIEZER, God our HELPER, I Declare that my heart will not be deceived, and I will not serve other gods.**

"Take heed to yourselves, that your heart be not deceived, and ye turn aside, and serve other gods, and worship them" (Deuteronomy 11:6).

19. **With Jehovah ELIEZER, God our HELPER, I Declare that the Word is nigh to me, in my mouth, and my heart.**

"But the word is very nigh unto thee, in thy mouth, and in thy heart, that thou mayest do it" (Deuteronomy 11:14).

20. **With Jehovah ELIEZER, God our HELPER, I Declare my heart rejoices in the LORD.**

And Hannah prayed, and said, My heart rejoices in the LORD, "mine horn is exalted in the LORD: my mouth is enlarged over mine enemies; because I rejoice in thy salvation." (1 Samuel 2:1).

21. **With Jehovah ELIEZER, God our HELPER, I Declare that God has given me another heart.**

"And it was so, that when he had turned his back to go from Samuel, God gave him another heart: and all those signs came to pass that day" (1 Samuel 10:9).

22. **With Jehovah ELIEZER, God our HELPER, I Declare will serve the LORD in truth with all my heart.**

"Only fear the LORD, and serve him in truth with all your heart: for consider how great things he hath done for you" (2 Samuel 12:24).

23. **With Jehovah ELIEZER, God our HELPER, I Declare I will do all that is in my heart according to His will.**

"And Nathan said to the king, Go, do all that is in thine heart; for the LORD is with thee" (2 Samuel 12:24).

24. **With Jehovah ELIEZER, God our HELPER, I Declare I have an understanding heart to judge justly.**

"Give therefore thy servant an understanding heart to judge thy people that I may discern between good and bad: for who is able to judge this thy so great a people?" (1 Kings 3:9).

25. **With Jehovah ELIEZER, God our HELPER, I Declare the LORD is nigh me because I have a heartbroken for Him.**

"The LORD is nigh unto them that are of a broken heart; and saveth such as be of a contrite spirit" (Psalm 34:18).

26. **With Jehovah ELIEZER, God our HELPER,**

I Declare my heart shall not fear because the LORD is my strength.

"Though an host should encamp against me, my heart shall not fear: though war should rise against me, in this will I be confident" (Psalm 27:3).

27. **With Jehovah ELIEZER, God our HELPER, I Declare God has created in me a clean heart.**

"Create in me a clean heart, O God; and renew a right spirit within me" (Psalm 51:10).

28. **With Jehovah ELIEZER, God our HELPER, I Declare my heart is fixed on Him.**

"My heart is fixed, O God, my heart is fixed: I will sing and give praise" (Psalm 51:7).

29. **With Jehovah ELIEZER, God our HELPER, I Declare my heart is united to fear God, and I will walk in truth.**

"Teach me thy way, O LORD; I will walk in thy truth: unite my heart to fear thy name" (Psalm 86:11).

30. **With Jehovah ELIEZER, God our HELPER, I Declare I will praise Him with my whole**

heart.

"I will praise thee with my whole heart: before the gods will I sing praise unto thee" (Psalm 138:1).

31. **With Jehovah ELIEZER, God our HELPER, I Declare I will trust in the LORD with all my heart; and not lean on my own understanding.**

    "Trust in the LORD with all thine heart; and lean not unto thine own understanding" (Proverbs 3:5).

32. **With Jehovah ELIEZER, God our HELPER, I Declare I will keep my heart with all diligence.**

    "Keep thy heart with all diligence; for out of it are the issues of life" (Proverbs 4:23).

33. **With Jehovah ELIEZER, God our HELPER, I Declare deferred hope will not make my heart sick, because desire, which is a tree of life, has come.**

    (Hope deferred maketh the heart sick: but when the desire cometh, it is a tree of life" (Proverbs 13:12).

34. **With Jehovah ELIEZER, God our HELPER, I Declare my heart is merry and has done me good like medicine.**

"A merry heart doeth good like a medicine: but a broken spirit drieth the bones" (Proverbs 17:22).

35. **With Jehovah ELIEZER, God our HELPER, I Declare I will apply my heart to instruction so I can gain knowledge.**

"Apply thine heart unto instruction, and thine ears to the words of knowledge" (Proverbs 23:12).

36. **With Jehovah ELIEZER, God our HELPER, I Declare my heart will not be proud. I will not stir up strife.**

"He that is of a proud heart stirreth up strife: but he that putteth his trust in the LORD shall be made fat" (Proverbs 28:25).

37. **With Jehovah ELIEZER, God our HELPER, I Declare that my heart will not be deceitful and wicked.**

"The heart is deceitful above all things, and desperately wicked: who can know it?"

(Jeremiah 17:9).

38. **With Jehovah ELIEZER, God our HELPER, I Declare I have a heart know to the LORD and return to Him wholly.**

   "And I will give them an heart to know Me, that I am the LORD: and they shall be my people, and I will be their God: for they shall return unto me with their whole heart" (Jeremiah 24:7).

39. **With Jehovah ELIEZER, God our HELPER, I Declare I have one heart and one way; that is to fear the LORD.**

   "And I will give them one heart, and one way that they may fear me forever, for the good of them, and of their children after them" (Jeremiah 32:39).

40. **With Jehovah ELIEZER, God our HELPER, I Declare that the fear of God is in my heart, and I will never depart from Him.**

   "And I will make an everlasting covenant with them, that I will not turn away from them, to do them good; but I will put my fear in their hearts, that they shall not depart from me" (Jeremiah 32:40).

41. **With Jehovah ELIEZER, God our HELPER, I Declare the heart of stone is removed, my heart is pliable that I may walk in His statutes and keep His ordinances.**

    *"And I will give them one heart, and I will put a new spirit within you; and I will take the stony heart out of their flesh, and will give them an heart of flesh: That they may walk in my statutes, and keep mine ordinances, and do them: and they shall be my people, and I will be their God" (*Ezekiel 11:19-20).

42. **With Jehovah ELIEZER, God our HELPER, I Declare I will lift up my heart with my hands to the LORD.**

    "Let us lift up our heart with our hands unto God in the heavens" (Lamentations 3:41).

43. **With Jehovah ELIEZER, God our HELPER, I Declare that the peace of God rules in my heart.**

    "And let the peace of God rule in your hearts, to which also ye are called in one body; and be ye thankful" (Colossians 3:15).

44. **With Jehovah ELIEZER, God our HELPER,**

I Declare that I draw near with a true heart in full assurance of faith, to the throne of grace.

"Let us draw near with a true heart in full assurance of faith, having our hearts sprinkled from an evil conscience, and our bodies washed with pure water" (Hebrews 10:22).

45. **With Jehovah ELIEZER, God our HELPER, I Declare that my heart does not condemn me; therefore, I know that God hears me, and I will have whatsoever I ask.**

"Beloved, if our heart condemn us not, then have we confidence toward God. And whatsoever we ask, we receive of Him, because we keep His commandments, and do those things that are pleasing in His sight" (1 John 3:21-22).

BATTLES OF THE WORLD WORLDLY VALUES AND PLEASURE-SEEKING LIFESTYLE.

46. **With Jehovah ELIEZER, God our HELPER, I Declare I am not conformed to this world, but I am transformed by the renewing of the mind by His Word.**

"And be not conformed to this world: but be ye transformed by the renewing of your mind, that

ye may prove what is that good, and acceptable, and perfect, will of God" (Romans 12:2).

47. With Jehovah ELIEZER, God our HELPER, I Declare I have not received the spirit of this world, but the Spirit of God so I know all things freely given to me.

"Now we have received, not the spirit of the world, but the spirit which is of God; that we might know the things that are freely given to us of God" (1 Corinthians 2:12).

48. With Jehovah ELIEZER, God our HELPER, I Declare I have not the wisdom of this world, which is foolishness with God.

"For the wisdom of this world is foolishness with God. For it is written, He taketh the wise in their own craftiness" (1 Corinthians 3:19).

49. With Jehovah ELIEZER, God our HELPER, I Declare I not lost because the god of this world has not blinded my mind from the light of the gospel.

"But if our gospel be hid, it is hid to them that are lost. In whom the god of this world hath blinded the minds of them which believe

not, lest the light of the glorious gospel of Christ, who is the image of God, should shine unto them" (2 Corinthians 4:3-4).

50. **With Jehovah ELIEZER, God our HELPER, I Declare I am delivered from this present evil world because Christ gave Himself for my sins.**

   "Who gave himself for our sins, that He might deliver us from this present evil world, according to the will of God and our Father" (Galatians 1:4).

51. **With Jehovah ELIEZER, God our HELPER, I Declare I no longer walk according to the course of this world, because Christ has quickened me from the death of sin.**

   "And you hath he quickened, who were dead in trespasses and sins; Wherein in time past ye walked according to the course of this world, according to the prince of the power of the air, the spirit that works in the children of disobedience" (Ephesians 2:1-2).

52. **With Jehovah ELIEZER, God our HELPER, I Declare I am blameless and harmless, and I shine as lights in this dark world.**

"Do all things without murmurings and disputing: That ye may be blameless and harmless, the sons of God, without rebuke, in the midst of a crooked and perverse nation, among whom ye shine as lights in the world" (Philippians 2:14-15).

53. **With Jehovah ELIEZER, God our HELPER, I Declare I will not be spoiled through philosophy and vain deceit and traditions of men, according to the world system.**

"Beware lest any man spoil you through philosophy and vain deceit, after the tradition of men, after the rudiments of the world, and not after Christ" (Colossians 2:8).

54. **With Jehovah ELIEZER, God our HELPER, I Declare when I ask, I will receive because I have no friendship with the world, and I am a friend of God.**

"Ye ask, and receive not, because ye ask amiss, that ye may consume it upon your lusts. Ye adulterers and adulteresses know ye not that the friendship of the world is enmity with God? Whosoever therefore will be a friend of the world

is the enemy of God" (James 4:3-4).

55. **With Jehovah ELIEZER, God our HELPER, I Declare I have overcome because the Greater One lives in me; Jesus Christ, the Son of The Living God.**

   "Ye are of God, little children, and have overcome them: because greater is He that is in you, than He that is in the world" (1 John 4:4).

56. **With Jehovah ELIEZER, God our HELPER, I Declare I have overcome the world because I am born of God, and this is the Victory that overcomes the world, even my faith.**

   "For whatsoever is born of God overcomes the world: and this is the victory that overcomes the world, even our faith" (1 John 5:4).

57. **With Jehovah ELIEZER, God our HELPER, I Declare I have overcome the world because I believe that Jesus is the Son of The Living God.**

   Who is he that overcomes the world, but he that believeth that Jesus is the Son of God? (1 John 5:5).

58. **With Jehovah ELIEZER, God our HELPER, I Declare I have victory in all Battles of PAST**

DISCOURAGEMENT.

"I press on, that I may lay hold of that which Christ Jesus has also laid hold of me. Forgetting those things which are behind and reaching forward to those things which are ahead, I press toward the goal for the prize of the upward call of God in Christ Jesus" (Philippians 3:12-14).

59. **With Jehovah ELIEZER, God our HELPER, I Declare I have victory in all Battles in my MARRIAGE.**

    "Marriage is honorable in all, and the bed undefiled: but whoremongers and adulterers God will judge" (Hebrews 13:4).

60. **With Jehovah ELIEZER, God our HELPER, I Declare I have victory in all Battles in my HEALTH.**

    "For I will restore health unto thee, and I will heal thee of thy wounds, saith the LORD; because they called thee an Outcast, saying, this is Zion, whom no man seeketh after" (Jeremiah 30:17).

61. **With Jehovah ELIEZER, God our HELPER, I Declare I have victory in all Battles with my CHILDREN.**

"And all thy children shall be taught of the LORD; and great shall be the peace of thy children" *(Isaiah 54:13).*

"Yea, thou shalt see thy children's children, and peace upon Israel" *(Psalm 128:6).*

62. **With Jehovah ELIEZER, God our HELPER, I Declare I have victory in all Battles in my FINANCES.**

    "Wealth and riches shall be in his house: and his righteousness endures forever" *(Psalm 12:3).*

63. **With Jehovah ELIEZER, God our HELPER, I Declare I have victory in all Battles in TEMPTATIONS.**

    "There hath no temptation taken you but such as is common to man: but God is faithful, who will not suffer you to be tempted above that ye are able; but will with the temptation also make a way to escape, that ye may be able to bear it" *(Corinthians 10:13).*

64. **With Jehovah ELIEZER, God our HELPER, I Declare I have victory in all Battles of WORRY.**

"I am anxious for nothing, but in everything by prayer and supplication with thanksgiving I let my requests be made known to God. And the peace of God, which surpasses all comprehension, will guard my hearts and minds in Christ Jesus" (*Philippians 4:6-7).*

65. **With Jehovah ELIEZER, God our HELPER, I Declare I have victory in all Battles of BARRENNESS.**

    "Thou shalt be blessed above all people: there shall not be male or female barren among you, or among your cattle" (*Deuteronomy 7:14).*

66. **With Jehovah ELIEZER, God, our HELPER, I Declare I have victory in all Battles HEALTH LUST AND SEXUAL IMPURITY.**

    "But among you there must not be even a hint of sexual immorality, or of any kind of impurity, or of greed, because these are improper for God's holy people" (*Ephesians 5:3).*

67. **With Jehovah ELIEZER, God our HELPER, I Declare I have victory in all Battles of POVERTY and LACK.**

"The young lions do lack, and suffer hunger: but they that seek the LORD shall not want any good thing" (Proverbs 34:10).

"I honor the Lord with my wealth and the first fruits of all my produce. Then, my barns will be filled with plenty. My vats will overflow with new wine" (Proverbs 3:9-10).

68. **With Jehovah ELIEZER, God our HELPER, I Declare I have victory in all Battles of GRIEF AND SORROW**

69. **With Jehovah ELIEZER, God our HELPER, I Declare I have victory in all Battles of UNFORGIVENESS because I choose to forgive.**

"And whenever you stand praying, if you have anything against anyone, forgive him that your Father in heaven may also forgive you your trespasses" (Mark 11:25).

I am kind and tenderhearted to others. I forgive them as God in Christ has forgiven me (Ephesians 4:32).

70. **With Jehovah ELIEZER, God our HELPER, I Declare The joy of the LORD is my strength**

(Nehemiah 8:10).

71. With Jehovah ELIEZER, God our HELPER, I Declare I am confident of this very thing, that He who has begun a good work in me will complete it until the day of Jesus Christ (Philippians 1:6).

72. With Jehovah ELIEZER, God our HELPER, I Declare God satisfies my mouth with good things and renews my youth like the eagles (Psalm 103:5).

73. With Jehovah ELIEZER, God our HELPER, I Declare I am God's masterpiece created in Christ Jesus, unto good works He planned for me long ago (Ephesians 2:10 NLT).

74. With Jehovah ELIEZER, God our HELPER, I Declare God does exceedingly abundantly above all that I could ask or think according to His power that works in me (Ephesians 3:20).

75. With Jehovah ELIEZER, God our HELPER, I Declare I am in Christ Jesus and therefore I am a new creation. Old things have passed away and all things have become new (2 Corinthians 5:17).

76. With Jehovah ELIEZER, God our HELPER, I Declare All of God's promises are yes and in Him Amen because I am in Christ (2 Corinthians 1:20).

77. With Jehovah ELIEZER, God our HELPER, I can confidently say, *"The Lord is my helper; I will not fear; what can man do to me?"* (Hebrews 13:6).

78. With Jehovah ELIEZER, God our HELPER, I can confidently say, *"His hand will help me fulfill my destiny because I have chosen His precepts. Let thine hand help me; for I have chosen thy precepts"* (Psalm 119:173).

79. With Jehovah ELIEZER, God our HELPER, I can confidently say, *"my help is in His matchless, powerful Name. Our help is in the name of the LORD, who made heaven and earth"* (Psalm 124:8).

In Jesus Name, Amen and Amen!

DAILY DECLARATIONS

You have the authority to decree a thing.

*"Thou shalt also **Decree** a thing, and it shall be established unto thee: and the light shall shine upon thy ways" (Job 22:28).*

Speak these declarations over your life DAILY with expectation:

I DECREE the keys of the kingdom of heaven have been given to me, and whatsoever I bind on earth is bound in heaven, and whatsoever I loose on earth is loosed in heaven (Matthew 16:19).

I DECREE no weapon formed against me shall prosper, and every tongue that shall rise against me in judgment shall be condemned (Isaiah 54:17).

I DECREE I am blessed coming in and blessed going out. I am the head and not the tail, above only, and not beneath (Deuteronomy 28:13).

I DECREE I am strong in the Lord and the power of His might as I put on the whole armor of God and stand against all the wiles of the devil (Ephesians 6:11).

I DECREE my steps are ordered every day by the Lord (Psalm 37:23).

I DECREE all things work together for my good because I love God and are called according to His purpose (Romans 8:28).

I DECREE God is my refuge and strength, a very present help in times of trouble (Psalms 46:1).

I DECREE God has not given me the spirit of fear, but of power, love, and a sound mind (2 Timothy 1:7).

I DECREE the LORD renews my strength; I mount up with wings as eagles; I run, and shall not be weary, walk, and faint not (Isaiah 40:31).

I DECREE the favor of God. If God be for me, who can be against me? (Romans 8:31).

I DECREE I give, and it shall be given back to me; good measure, pressed down, shaken together, and running over, shall men give into my bosom (Luke 6:38).

I DECREE I delight myself in the LORD, and he gives me the desires of my heart (Psalms 37:4).

I DECREE I have the peace of God that passes all understanding (Philippians 4:7).

I DECREE I am a believer with signs follow me. In the Name of Jesus, I cast out devils, speak with new tongues, take up serpents, and if I drink any deadly thing, it will not harm me; I lay hands on the sick, and they recover (Mark 16:17-19).

I DECREE greater is He that lives in me than he that lives in the world (1 John 4:4).

I DECREE My God supplies all of my needs according to His riches in glory by Christ Jesus (Philippians 4:19).

I DECREE by His stripes; I am healed (1 Peter 2:24).

I DECREE I am born of God, and the evil one cannot touch me (1 John 5:18).

I DECREE I call on the Lord, and He answers me and shows me great and mighty things I know not of (Jeremiah 33:3).

I DECREE I have been given the power to tread on serpents and scorpions, and overall the power of the enemy: and nothing shall by any means hurt me. (Luke 10:19)

I DECREE God gives me the treasures of darkness and hidden riches of secret places that I may know that the LORD is God. (Isaiah 45:3)

I DECREE God is not a man that he should lie to me, neither the son of man that he should change His mind. The things he has said, he will do, and the things he has spoken he will make good. (Numbers 23:19)

I DECREE wealth and riches shall be in my house because I fear the Lord. (Psalm 112:3)

I DECREE the kingdom of God come, in my life, family, marriage, ministry, relationships, and work. (Matthew 6:10)

I DECREE I am satisfied with the words of my mouth because life and death are in the power of my tongue. Proverbs 18:20

I DECREE, with absolute faith by God's eternal Spirit of grace and mercy that I now inhabit heavenly places and sit high above all principality and power, might and dominions and every name that is named! Thus, I work, walk, talk, and think in authority and exercise my right to be rich and live the abundant lifestyle given unto me by Christ Jesus, in Jesus' name (Ephesians 1:12-23, 2:4).

I DECREE with absolute faith that today going forward. I operate outside this world's system and accumulate wealth, health, riches, honor, and blessing supernaturally by divine providence, favor, mercy, in Jesus' name!

(Philippians 4:19).

I DECREE with absolute faith that as an heir of God and joint-heir with Christ I have a right to be rich, prosperous and well satisfied in all areas of my life with plenty to give and enough to meet all needs that arise with plenty to spare, in Jesus' name (2 Corinthians 9:6-12)

I DECREE with absolute faith that the divine will of God is for me to dwell in my wealthy place! Multiple channels of prosperity, riches, health, wealth, abundance, and financial increase come into, invade and saturate my life now in Jesus' name! Deuteronomy 28:1-14

I DECREE with absolute faith that my hearing is acute, fine-tuned, bent toward His heart and magnetized to the voice of the Holy Spirit who shall speak to me, lead and guide me into my wealthy place. Thus, I will trust, follow, and execute the plans of the Spirit to achieve my destination and inhabit this fabulous place (Isaiah 48:15-18).

I DECREE with absolute faith that I have arrived in my wealthy place of abundance, prosperity, riches, spiritual power, wisdom, and blessing!

The blessing of Abraham has exploded in my life, and I now have become a channel for God's unlimited flow of supplies and a vessel prepared for His use, n Jesus' name (Psalm 66:12, 2 Peter 1:3-11, Galatians 3:13-14).

I DECREE with absolute faith that God is my source using many channels, of which I am one, to bless His people and accomplish His will in the earth realm.

As a channel, I open myself up to receive and release by faith, healing, empowerment, salvation, wisdom, knowledge, creative ideas, increase, blessing, the anointing, discernment, love, reconciliation, restoration, deliverance, stability, and grace all, in Jesus' name (Isaiah 60).

I DECREE with absolute faith that I let the wisdom of God overshadow my spirit, mind, soul, and body that I may be guided in what to say, how to say it and to whom to say it to, in Jesus' name (Isaiah 55:11-13).

I DECREE with absolute faith that every day I expect, experience, and manifest the miracles of the kingdom, which validate, vindicate, and confirm the Word of God in the earth realm (Psalm 62:5).

I DECREE with absolute faith that I walk, operate, pray, and speak through the Spirit. I see, hear, and manifest the things of the Spirit through the fruit and gifts of the Spirit of God. Through my spiritual connection with the *righteousness, judgment, and Kingdom* of God, I receive, I am entitled to, and embrace the prepared blessings that have been reserved, revealed, transferred and released into my life, family, and church (1 Corinthians 2:9-12).

I DECREE with absolute faith that today forward, I believe all things are possible through the anointing, the Word, and recognizing God as my source (Luke 1:37).

I DECREE with absolute faith that today, my heart is filled with the presence of God and will forever provide a place for His habitation, demonstration, and power! (2 Corinthians 4:7).

I DECREE with absolute faith that I walk under the anointing of Christ, which has destroyed all yokes, links, chains, and strongholds connected to my life and all those I connect with. Setting all completely, free financially, physically, spiritually, and emotionally (Isaiah 10:27, Jonah 8:32,36, 2 Corinthians 10:3-6).

I DECREE with absolute faith that today I flow in the anointing of Christ, the grace of God, and empowerment of the Holy Spirit for the fulfillment of His will for my life and advancement of humanity, family, and the kingdom. (Isaiah 11:1-4, Luke 10:19-20, Acts 1:8).

I DECREE with absolute faith that the spirit of fear,

doubt, unbelief, disobedience, and deception are broken and eliminated from my life, family, ministry, and church. Thus, I now flow with the Trinity in peace, power, wisdom, understanding, knowledge, gifts, skills, talents of the Kingdom of God for the manifestation of His Glory in the earth realm (John 7:38-39, 16:13-16).

I DECREE with absolute faith that from this day forward, I'll never be broke again another day of my life. The anointing has destroyed all yokes, chains, hindrances, restrictions, obstacles, and dams that have blocked all forms of increase, prosperity, advancement, elevations, and promotions that were ordained for the fulfillment of God's will in my life, family, and church (Isaiah 10:27, 2 Corinthians 8:9).

I DECREE with absolute faith that the Lord is my shepherd and I shall not want! He restores my soul, anoints my head, mind, and spirit and makes my soul over ow with joy, peace, power, the anointing, love, vision, dreams, directions, favor, and patience (Psalm 23).

I DECREE with absolute faith that I through, the anointing of God shall not want, have, lack, experience poverty or suffer need but shall be completely supplied with all blessings both natural and spiritual to fulfill my destiny! Thus, I attract abundance in all forms, experience financial freedom, and become a lender, the head above only, and obtain all resources from God my only source, in the form of gifts, donations, rewards, grants, business transactions, miracles, divine manifestations, wealth transfers and the like that I may excel, advance the Kingdom of God, and establish His covenant in the earth realm and bring Glory to His name (1 Chronicles 29:11-12, Deuteronomy 28:1-14).

I DECREE, with absolute faith, that today supernatural debt cancellation has taken place in my life, ministry, family and church, wealth, riches, prosperity, all currencies, and financial elevation comes into my life now without delay, in Jesus' name (Genesis 12:1-3, 13:1-2).

I DECREE with absolute faith that today, this is my DECADE of DESTINY DELIVERY AND DESTINY FULFILLMENT, IN JESUS' NAME! AMEN!

Your Covenant Commitment to the Ministry

1. PRAY daily for at least 15 minutes.
2. PRAY daily for divine protection for my family and me, as well as for our worldwide ministry team and their families, and our entire ministry.
3. PRAY daily for a harvest of souls around the world.
4. PRAY daily for your nation, its government, your church leaders, and for spiritual revival.
5. PRAY daily for the urgent prayer requests that come to the ministry from God's people around the globe.
6. PRAY daily for the other prayer warriors in this mighty army.
7. PRAISE God daily for the victories He is pouring upon the lives of His people.

Our Covenant Commitment to You

1. My team and I promise to pray daily for you and your loved ones.
2. You will be able to submit your prayer requests and praise reports directly to my private e-mail address explicitly reserved for members of the Prayer Academy, Elite Warriors.
3. We will stand in the gap on your behalf until you get the victory.
4. We will send you e-mails for special events that are occurring, as well as urgent prayer requests from people around the globe.

Prayer Declaration Series by Sarah Morgan

1. Activating and Affirming God's Prophecies and Promises
2. Affirmations of Faith
3. Blessed State of the Righteous
4. Breaking the Anti-Marriage Spirit
5. Breaking Dream Killers
6. Chain Breakers
7. Children's Prayers
8. Cleansing from Defilement
9. Destroying the Spirit of Stagnancy
10. Finances-Prosperity
11. Healing Prayer
12. Healing is for You
13. I Am Declarations
14. Praying by the Blood of Jesus
15. Prayers for Healing
16. Prayer for Husbands
17. Prophetic Call
18. Pursue and Overtake and Recover
19. Seven Mountain Prayer
20. Supernatural God
21. The Snare is Broken
22. Waiting on the Faithfulness and Loving Kindness of God
23. Weapons of Mass Destruction I
24. Weapons of Mass Destruction II
25. Wisdom
26. Eliezer Lord My Helper
27. When You Pray Not If
28. Quantum Prayer Leap Decrees

ADDITIONAL BOOKS BY DR. SARAH MORGAN

1. 7 Days of Fasting and Prayer
2. 21 Days of Fasting and Prayer
3. 30 Days of Fasting and Prayer
4. Confessing the Proverbs
5. Declaring the Psalms
6. Intercession by Pattern
7. Prayer the Master Key Revised Edition
8. Sing O' Barren Revised Edition
9. Seed of a Women
10. The Prayer Factor
11. The Faith Factor
12. You Shall Decree a Thing

To Sponsor a Prayer Academy Seminar in your city, to invite Sarah Morgan to your next conference, service, encounter, Revival, Crusade, or for additional information, please contact the Prayer Academy administrative offices.

To enroll or for additional information regarding **Prayer Academy University (PAU)**, please visit www.prayeracademy.university

Contact Information:
Email: admin@prayeracademyglobal.com
Phone: 1-888-320-5622 ext.1

ABOUT THE AUTHOR

SARAH MORGAN is skillful, prolific, insightful, and balanced in the teaching of God's word and mightily used in the gifts of the Holy Spirit. Sarah Morgan is an anointed and appointed vessel of God who has shaken the community of Los Angeles and abroad. She has been honored with several awards that recognize her contributions to the community, influence in leadership, and examples of accomplishments and sacrifice for family and friends. She is the Chancellor of Prayer Academy University, and she facilitates Prayer Academy Seminars, conferences, and retreats, which serve to equip, empower and transform ministry leaders from "Doctrine to Demonstration" with the mandate to preserve the Legacy of Prayer in the church.

Sarah Morgan's ministry is sought after and has taken her to South, East and West Africa, London, and across the United States. Everywhere she goes, the power of God within her is demonstrated as the atmosphere changes in her presence, and forces in existence move back to accommodate the Word of God.

Made in the USA
Columbia, SC
02 November 2023